Numbers

This book
belongs to

_____

FS109004 • Numbers

One Amazing Mouse

Trace and write.

FS109004 • Numbers

One by One

Color every object that has a **1** on it.

FS109004 • Numbers

Two Terrific Turtles

2

Trace and write.

2 2 2

A Pair Is Two

Color every object that has a **2** on it.

FS109004 • Numbers

Three Incredible Kites

3

Trace and write.

3 3 3

FS109004 • Numbers

On the Fly

Color every bird that has a **3** on it.

FS109004 • Numbers

Four Fun Friends

Trace and write.

Monkey Around

Color **brown** every space that has a 4 in it.
Color the other spaces **green**.

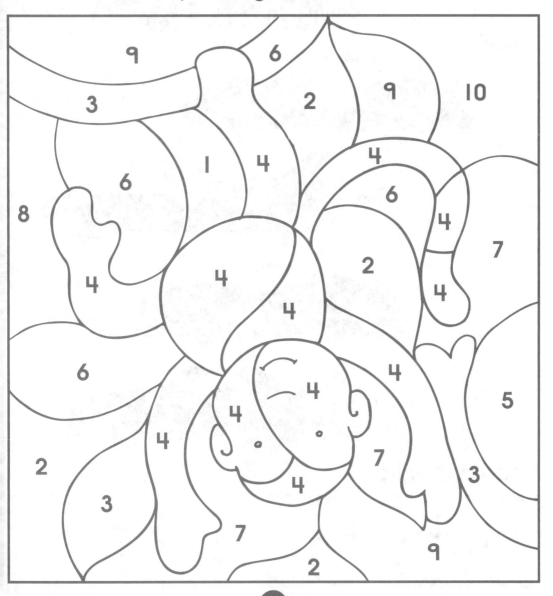

FS109004 • Numbers

Five Fast Cars

5

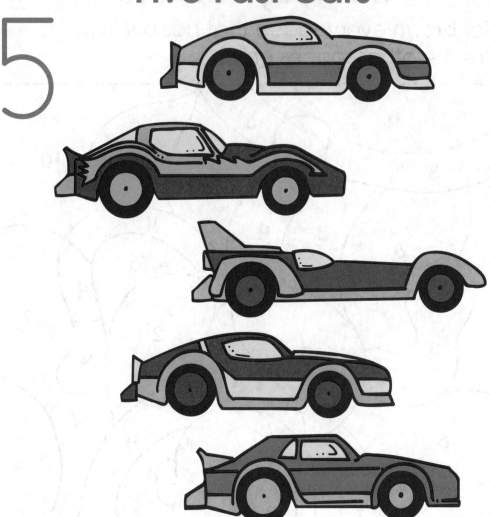

Trace and write.

5 5 5

   FS109004 • Numbers

Drive With 5

Color every driver wearing a **5**.

Six Super Scooters

6

Trace and write.

6 6 6

FS109004 • Numbers

The Search for 6

Circle every 6.

Seven Bouncing Balls

7

Trace and write.

    FS109004 • Numbers

Silly Seals

Color **7** seals.

FS109004 • Numbers

Eight Awesome Ants

8

Trace and write.

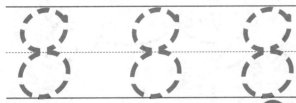

       FS109004 • Numbers

Great 8!

Color every space that has an **8** on it **red**.
Color every space that has a **3** on it yellow.

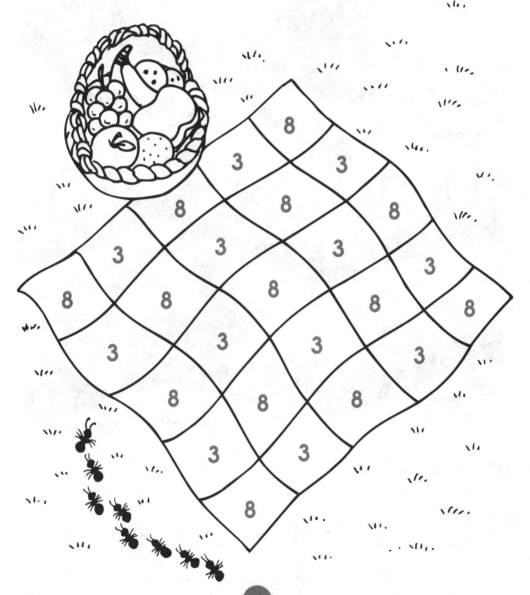

Nine Nifty Nests

Trace and write.

Sweet Baby Birds

Color every baby bird that has a 9 on it.

FS109004 • Numbers

Ten Fantastic Fish

10

Trace and write.

10 10

FS109004 • Numbers

Fishing for Tens

Color every fish that has a **10** on it.

FS109004 • Numbers

Hard Workers

Color 1 bulldozer.

Lots of Teeth

Color **2** alligators.

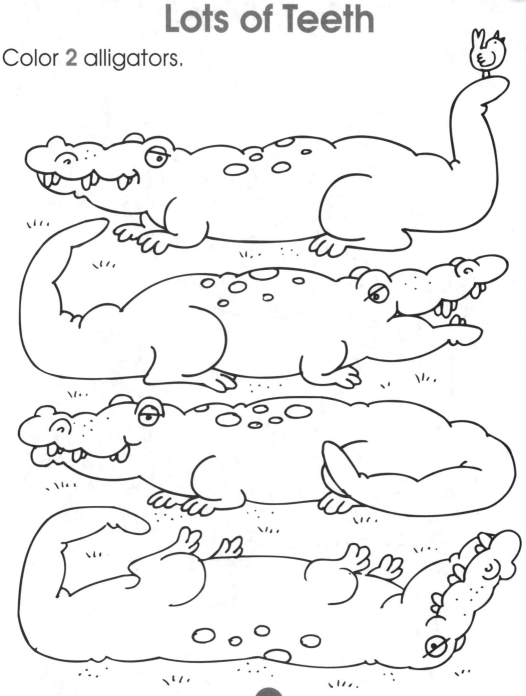

FS109004 • Numbers

Big Talkers

Color **3** birds.

FS109004 • Numbers

A Little Nutty

Color 4 squirrels.

Pretty Flowers

Color **5** flowers.

A Bunch of Balls

Color **6** balls.

© Carson-Dellosa   FS109004 • Numbers

Puppies

Color **7** puppies.

Good Job!

Color **8** prizes.

Happy Hearts

Color **9** hearts.

FS109004 • Numbers

Funny Frogs

Color **10** frogs.

Very Good Veggies

Circle the correct number in each box.

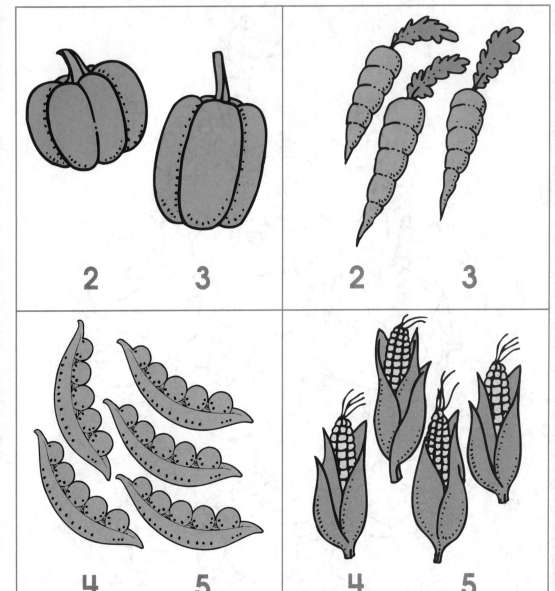

2   3

2   3

4   5

4   5

32

Fantastic Fruit

Circle the correct number in each box.

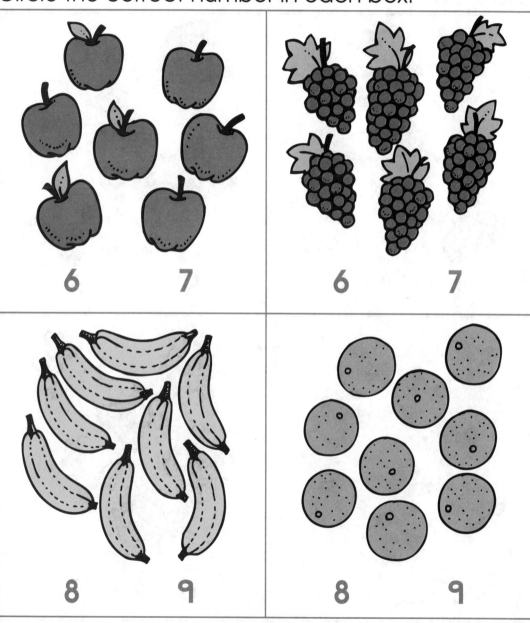

6   7

6   7

8   9

8   9

Fishy Fun

Circle the correct number in each box.

2 3

4 5

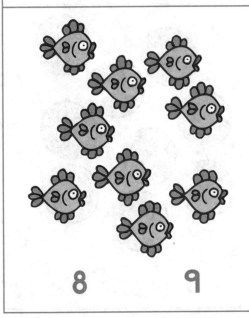

8 9

6 7

FS109004 • Numbers

Don't Bug Me!

Circle the correct number in each box.

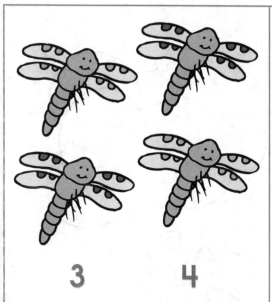

3   4

1   2

4   5

7   8

Rolling Along

A ride in this is always fun!

Connect the dots from **1** to **5**.

FS109004 • Numbers

Hats for All

Circle **2**.

Circle **4**.

Circle **3**.

Circle **5**.

Unfinished Flowers

Draw petals to finish the flowers.
Color.

Draw **3**.

Draw **2**.

Draw **5**.

Draw **1**.

        FS109004 • Numbers

Sweet Treats

Circle **7**.

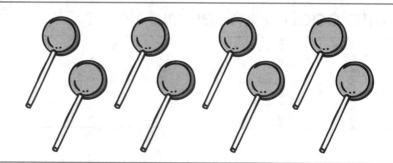

Circle **6**.

Circle **9**.

Circle **8**.

FS109004 • Numbers

Let's Write

Write each number four times.

1

2   2

3   3

4   4

5   5

FS109004 • Numbers

Write Some More

Write each number three times.

What a Trunk!

This huge animal has big ears and a long trunk.

Connect the dots from **1** to **10**.

Write the numbers from **1** to **5**.

_____

- -

_____

How Many?

Count the objects in each set.
Write the number on the line.

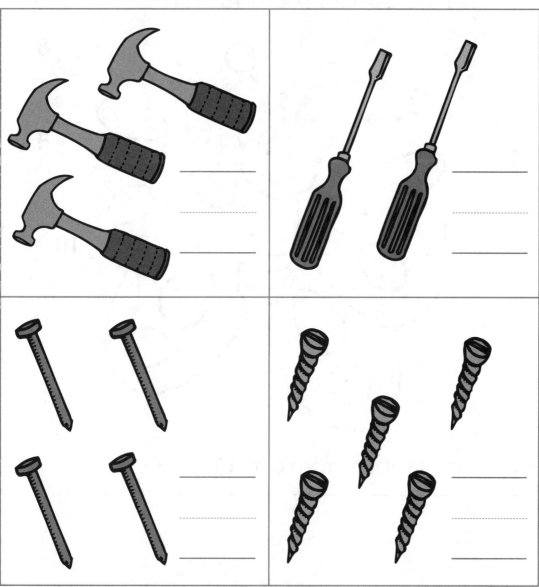

Light and Pretty

You can see this flying around flowers in the spring.

Connect the dots from **1** to **10**.

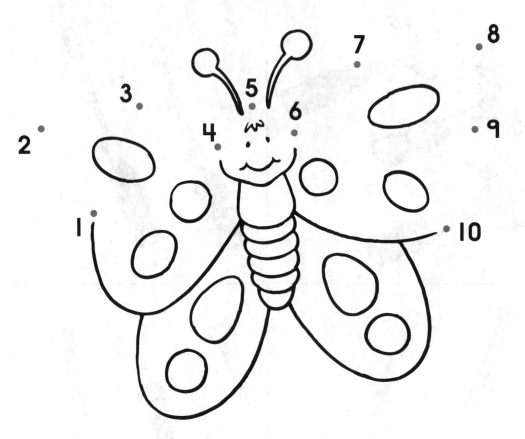

Write the numbers from **6** to **10**.

Look and Count

Count the objects in each set.
Write the number on the line.

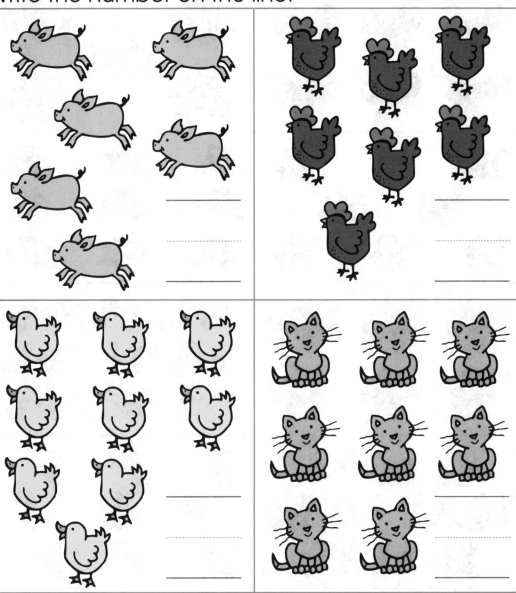

FS109004 • Numbers

Find More

In each row, circle the set that has more.

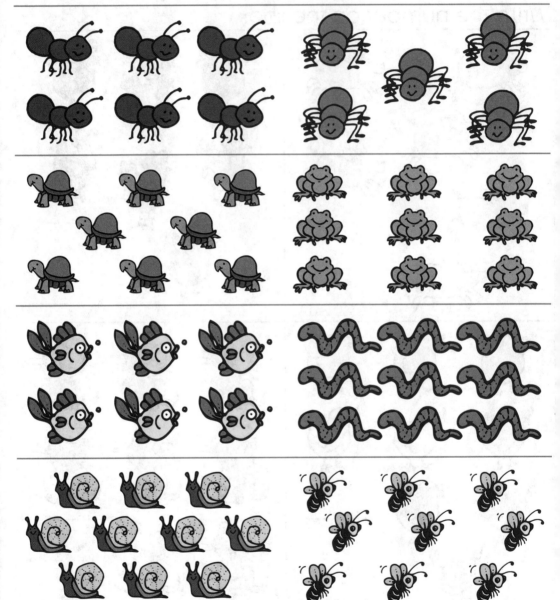

© Carson-Dellosa · FS109004 • Numbers

Find Less

In each row, circle the set that has fewer.

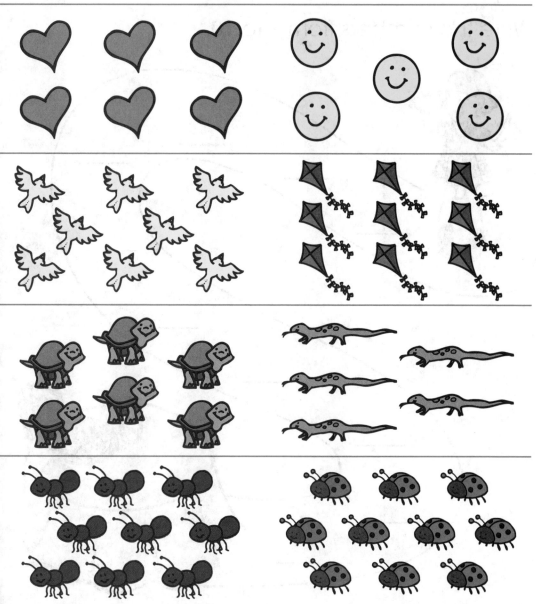

    FS109004 • Numbers

Write by Heart

Help Janie find the cookies.

Write the numbers from 1 to 10.

FS109004 • Numbers

Number Words

Read and trace.

1	one	one
2	two	two
3	three	three
4	four	four
5	five	five

FS109004 • Numbers

Match Them

Draw a line from each number to its number word.

Outdoor Fun

Circle **five**.

Circle **one**.

Circle **four**.

Circle **three**.

Circle **two**.

FS109004 • Numbers

More Number Words

Read and trace.

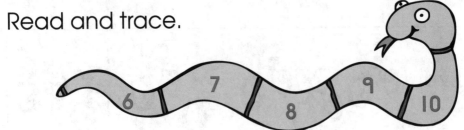

6   six   six

7   seven   seven

8   eight   eight

9   nine   nine

10   ten   ten

FS109004 • Number

Match Again

Draw a line from each number to its number word.

On the Move

Circle **six**.

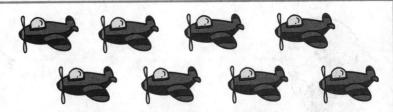

Circle **ten**.

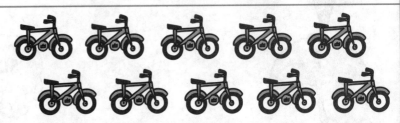

Circle **seven**.

Circle **nine**.

Circle **eight**.

FS109004 • Number

Duck Bath

This duckling cools off when it is hot.
Connect the dots from **1** to **10**.

FS109004 • Numbers

_____

knows all about numbers!

_____
signature

_____
date

FS109004 • Numbers